KNOW
YOUR
KNOTS

Bath • New York • Cologne • Melbourne • Delhi
Hong Kong • Shenzhen • Singapore • Amsterdam

This edition published by Parragon Books Ltd in 2014
and distributed by

Parragon Inc.
440 Park Avenue South, 13th Floor
New York, NY 10016
www.parragon.com

Text by Geoffrey Budworth
Knot diagrams by Malcolm Porter
Knot photography by Roddy Paine
Designed by Design Principals

ISBN 978-1-4723-4684-1

Printed in China

WARNING
This book is a simple
introduction to knot tying.
Do not use any of the knots,
bends, and hitches featured
for activities involving
predictable risk of loss,
damage, or injury, until you
have first sought the advice
and guidance of qualified
practitioners and obtained
from them appropriate
training and equipment.

Never loop ropes, or tie knots,
around the neck of anyone
and always ensure that
lengths of rope and cord are
safely coiled and stored out
of the reach of children.

Contents

Introduction   4

Knot names and terms   6

MULTIPURPOSE KNOTS

Sheepshank   8

Constrictor knot   10

Hoisting hitch   12

Tarbuck knot   14

Reef knot (reinforced)   16

LIFE-SUPPORT KNOTS

Alpine butterfly loop   18

Tape knot   19

Figure-eight loop   20

Reever bend   22

Figure-eight bend (reinforced)   23

BOATING KNOTS

Bowline   24

Carrick bend   26

Figure-eight becket hitch   27

Figure-eight stopper knot   28

Round turn and two half hitches   30

Fisherman's bend   31

Glossary of terms & Index   32

Introduction

There is no other field of human activity where we happily teach techniques that are thousands of years old ... Every other human endeavor has changed drastically over the centuries, but we still rely on many of the same techniques in knotting as those used by our distant ancestors.

(Richard Hopkins, *Knots*, 2003)

Everyone should know how to tie a knot or two ... or ten. If you cannot yet do so, that is merely because you have not learned how. And now is the best time to remedy this omission, as knotting has become a lively field of endeavor, keenly pursued by an increasing number of devotees of both sexes and all ages.

Nobody should be totally reliant upon factory-made clips, clamps, clasps, and any other gadgets, when a knotted lace or lashing will do at least as well—often better. For this reason knot tyers, a resourceful and self-sufficient lot, are rarely without cord in their pockets.

Learn only a handful of the knots described in this book, use them often, and you will become a different person. As a knotting aficionado you will never be at a loss when faced with needing to apply a life-saving, first aid tourniquet,

attaching a towline to a broken-down vehicle, or flying a kite on a string. Astronauts and zoologists (and every trade or calling alphabetically in-between) ought to know the ropes and how to knot them.

Anyway, all practicalities aside, knotting is an enjoyable recreation, as absorbing as doing a jigsaw puzzle or solving a crossword. Knotting is also a creative pastime, and skilled knotters can use their expertise to produce stunning artwork, decoration, and jewelry, from cord and string.

Because a disproportionate number of the brain's neural connections are involved with tasks requiring manual dexterity, knotting can also be therapeutic. The recovery of several stroke victims, for example, is said to have been helped by the practice of tying knots.

Knotting can be an art, a craft, and a science (all beyond the scope of this introductory book) about which we may still know less than half of what remains to be discovered. Knot theory is a subfield of topology (multidimensional geometry) and, in 1990, the New Zealand professor Vaughan Jones, FRS, was awarded a Fields Medal—the mathematicians' equivalent of a Nobel Prize—for his fruitful research in this abstruse and esoteric area, where the Jones polynomial has become a useful tool.

KNOTS AND NAMES
Most knots are multi purpose and separating them into different sections results in some arbitrary decisions. Do not be misled. Many—if not all—of those grouped together as Boating Knots and Life-Support Knots would be just as effective doing other things.

Knot names and terms

Alpine butterfly loop, figure-eight loop, and Carrick bend—are they Olympic figure-skating maneuvers, or the latest diabolical computer viruses? In fact, they are knot names. Knotting is a craft which has its own helpful—but highly specialized—jargon.

There are thousands of different knots and uncountable variations of some kinds of them. All, however, can be allocated into one of three main groups, namely:

- **Bends** which join the separate ends of ropes or cords in such a way that they can be untied later
- **Hitches** attaching one end of a line to a rail, ring, spar, or post (or another rope)
- **Knots** which include anything that is not a bend or hitch

The all-embracing label "knot" brings together fixed loops, adjustable or slide-and-grip nooses, bindings, shortenings, and stopper knots.

You do not need to know the name of any individual knot in order to learn and use it, but it helps to know their names when talking with other knot tyers, and becomes essential when reading and writing about them. Knotty nomenclature can, however, help or hinder.

A knot's name may suggest its:
- appearance (figure-eight stopper knot, round turn and two half hitches)
- use (hoisting hitch)
- user (fisherman's bend).

A name may imply—rightly or wrongly:
- the region of origin (Alpine butterfly loop)
- originator (Carrick bend).

Some knots have evocative names, while several have over time acquired more than one designation.

NOTE

The standing part of any rope used to be called "the bight," which is why knots in the middle of a rope—made without using either end—are still said to be "tied in the bight." Today, however, the term "bight" tends to be limited to a doubled, U-shaped tongue of rope or cord. Although bights at the end of a line may have knots tied in them, this is NOT, strictly speaking, tying in the bight ... it is merely tying with a bight or the doubled end of a line. Knots tied in the bight, strictly speaking, do not need ends. Confusing? Well, part of the fun in learning knots is picking up such arcane fragments of knot lore.

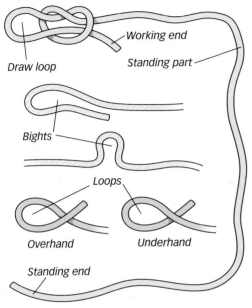

"Slipped" overhand or thumb knot

Working end

Draw loop

Standing part

Bights

Loops

Overhand

Underhand

Standing end

Tying terms *(see diagram above)*

Pick up a length of rope or cord to make any knot and the end with which you tie that knot is termed the **working end**. The other inert end is the **standing end**. Everything between these two extremes is the **standing part**.

Impart a half-twist to a bight and the result is a **loop**. Loops may be **overhand** (when the working end is placed on top) or **underhand** (when it lies underneath).

A knot impatiently or carelessly tightened will be a weak and unreliable knot. Tightening is as important as the tying process and should be performed with as much thought and care. Only a few knots (for instance, the double reef bows in shoelaces) can be tightened by simply tugging. Most knots must first be **dressed**, that is, molded into their final form with one's fingertips. Only then can tightening begin with careful removal of slack and daylight from the knot by pulling, a bit at a time, upon each end or strand that emerges from the knot to bed it down. Finally, when each turn and tuck is snug and neat, give each end and strand a parting tug to conclude the tightening process.

Buying cordage

The only stuff you need with which to learn and practice the knots featured in this book is a couple of 6-ft 6-in (2-m) lengths of braided cord no more than ⅓ in (between 5–10 mm) in diameter. They should be soft-laid, and they could be different colors.

If you buy anything else for some practical purpose, then bear in mind that (comparing like with like) a thicker rope is stronger than a thinner one, twice as thick being four times as strong. Braids are stronger than strands, and synthetic cordage is stronger and more durable than natural fiber—so it can be thinner. Do not buy cordage that is bigger and better quality—and consequently more expensive—than you need for the job in hand.

Sheepshank

This underrated knot is, in fact, quite versatile. It can shorten a rope or long cord without cutting it, and so preserve it intact for reuse another time; or it will, temporarily, bridge a damaged and weakened section of a rope until it can be replaced. A rudimentary sheepshank suspends bell ropes tidily and safely in a church belfry when not required, and the same knot forms the cordage purchase, applied in bygone days by carters to lash down loads securely, known today as the "trucker's hitch."

1 Cast a trio of loops—
two of them overhand,
the third underhand—with
the middle one bigger
than the others.

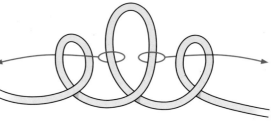

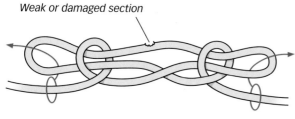

Weak or damaged section

2 Pull the left-hand leg of
the central loop out through
the nearest smaller loop,
going over-under. Similarly,
pull the right-hand loop leg
out through its adjacent
smaller loop, going under-
over.

3 Finally, lock off the end loops in one of two ways:
either pull the standing part of the line right the way
through, creating a layout similar to that of the bowline
(see page 24;) or trap the standing part against the end
loop with an improvised toggle that could be a length
of wooden doweling, a
screwdriver, a wrench,
or anything else of
the right size and
rigidity.

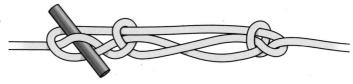

KNOT LORE
It is most unlikely that this knot was ever used to tether sheep while they grazed; but it may be that the knot was named for its resemblance to one of that creature's leg bones.

Constrictor knot

The constrictor is a tenacious binding knot, applied to the cut ends of ropes as a first-aid alternative to whipping. It will hold a hose on a faucet or keep joinery joints together while the glue dries, and can even be used to tether a pencil or ballpoint pen to a clipboard.

Method 1 (tying with an end)

1 To tie a constrictor to a ring or long rail, first take a turn with the working end and lead it diagonally over itself from SW to NE. Take a second turn and tuck the end beneath the diagonal.

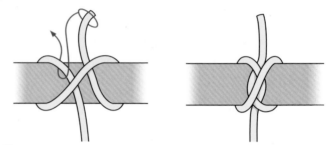

2 Finally, take the working end to tie a simple half-knot with the standing end. Tighten the knot by pulling on both ends, so that the overriding diagonal pins and holds the half-knot. The ends may be cut off close to the knot for extra neatness.

Method 2 (Where possible, tie a constrictor "in the bight," that is, without using an end)

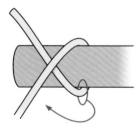

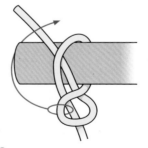

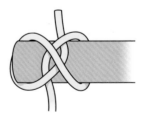

1 First slip a turn onto the rope's end or whatever else is to be seized.

2 Next, pull out a bight from the lower part of that turn.

3 Half-twist the loop and place over the end. Tighten the knot and trim off both ends.

KNOT LORE
There is documentary evidence that a knot resembling the constrictor—and perhaps identical to it—was used in ancient Greece as a surgical sling.

Hoisting hitch

This rope holdfast will help you to raise sections of drainpipe or guttering aloft; haul felled tree trunks and lopped branches over rough terrain; tow flotsam and salvaged items through water; and, in smaller cordage, it can be used to haul heavy hand tools up to elevated work levels where they are required.

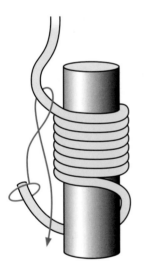

1 Wrap six to eight turns, working away from the end of the object to be lifted.

2 Bring the working end diagonally upwards (in this instance, from SW to NE) and take it around behind the standing part of the rope or cord (from right to left).

3 Finally, take a turn with the working end and lock it off with a half hitch.

EXPERT TIP
Carefully tighten every turn and tuck of this knot, then repeat the process, before loading it.

KNOT LORE
This knot was known and used by American tree surgeons (who called it "the squeeze knot") in Wisconsin during the 1940s; but it was popularized in the UK during the 1950s by British climbing writer Ken Tarbuck—after whom it is named.

Tarbuck knot

This slide-and-grip loop knot or noose is ideal for guy ropes on tents and marquees or garden awnings, and for other types of stays and shrouds (for instance, to brace a windbreak on the beach at the seaside), which may from time to time need to be adjusted.

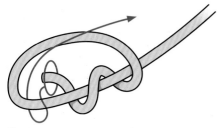

1 Form an overhand loop and then tuck the working end twice through and around itself.

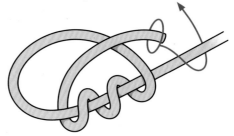

2 Next, take the working end up and around behind the standing part of the line from right to left.

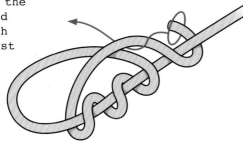

3 Then tuck the end over and down through the loop just made.

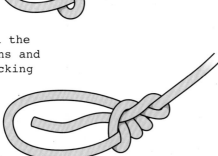

4 Tighten all the wrapping turns and the final locking tuck with care before loading the knot.

EXPERT TIP
Grasp the knot and slide it along until the loop is the required size. When loaded, it will hold firm by creating a dog-leg deformation in the standing part of the line. Remove the load and it can be readjusted.

Reef knot (reinforced)

As sails are rarely reefed by means of cord "reef points" these days, the knot now described has not been located in the section on Boating Knots. Astonishingly (in view of the Expert tip comments), it is actually recommended in one or two climbing manuals for joining two or more abseil (or rappel) lines to one another.

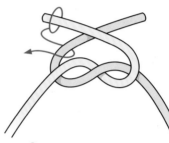

1 Cross the two lines, left-over-right, and tie a half-knot.

2 Cross them again, right-over-left, and add a second half-knot.

3 The resulting flat knot, consisting of two interlocked bights, is termed an SZ knot (because of the lay or handedness of each half-knot, in the order they were tied).

4 The mirror-image reef knot is a ZS version.

5 Never use a reef knot as a bend without backing up or locking off both ends. Leave the ends long enough to stitch, tape, or tie them (with a pair of double overhand knots, as illustrated) to their adjacent standing parts.

EXPERT TIP
Beware—the naked reef knot (not reinforced) is notoriously weak, reducing the breaking strength of any rope or cord in which it is tied by 50 per cent or more. It is merely a binding knot, fit only to tie around the necks of duffel bags and garbage bags, or for packages, bandages, and shoe-laces (in the form of a double reef bow).

Alpine butterfly loop

This classic climbing knot—tied in the bight, without using either end—forms a fixed loop for the middle member of a team (in glacier travel, for instance) to clip into with a karabiner. It will withstand a pull from any direction. The knot can also be used to bridge a damaged and weakened part of a rope.

1 Make a closed bight in the rope and impart a twist of 180º.

2 Invert the upper loop, bringing it down in front of the lower loop to lie on the two legs of the bight.

3 Then pull the lower loop up through the central compartment, from back to front, and tighten the resulting knot.

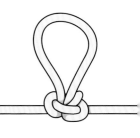

Tape knot

This is the only bend recommended by climbing councils and clubs to join two lengths of webbing (although it works well in cordage too), and it is an alternative to the figure-eight bend described later in this section. This knot is also known as the "ring bend" or "overhand bend."

1 In the end of one length of webbing, tie a simple overhand or thumb knot.

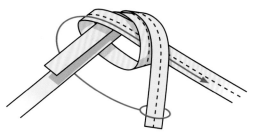

2 Insert the end of the second piece of webbing and start to follow around the original knot.

3 When the first knot has been completely traced and doubled, tighten the resulting bend.

Figure-eight loop

This knot is widely preferred for tying a fixed loop into the end of a rope, because it is easy to learn and then recall in the most challenging of circumstances. Fasten it to inanimate anchorages and secure belayed climbers with it.

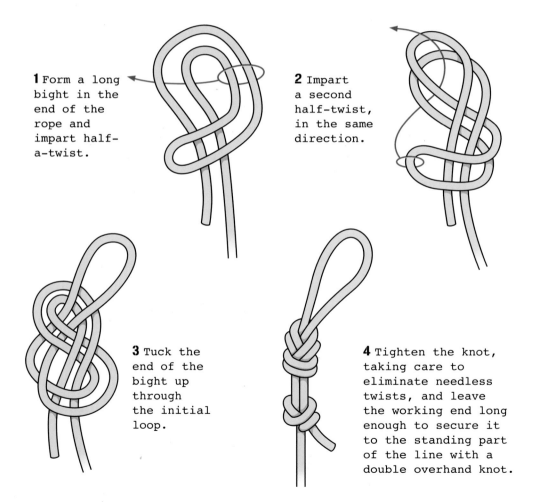

1 Form a long bight in the end of the rope and impart half-a-twist.

2 Impart a second half-twist, in the same direction.

3 Tuck the end of the bight up through the initial loop.

4 Tighten the knot, taking care to eliminate needless twists, and leave the working end long enough to secure it to the standing part of the line with a double overhand knot.

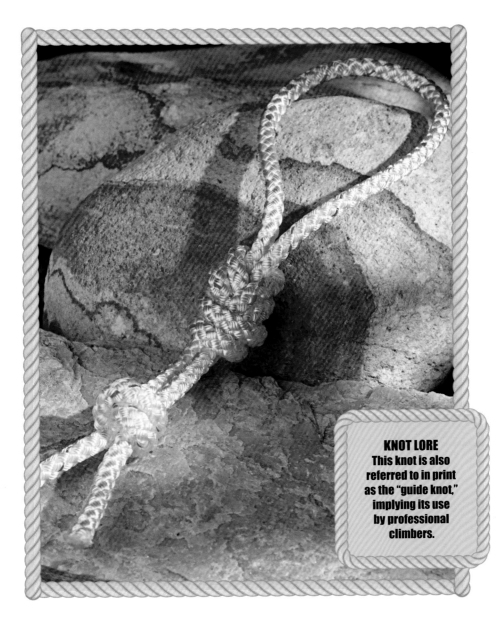

KNOT LORE
This knot is also referred to in print as the "guide knot," implying its use by professional climbers.

Reever bend

Join two ropes together with this strong and secure bend. They should be of similar diameter and construction, although a reever bend will work quite well with a couple of dissimilar ropes or cords.

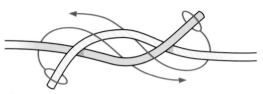

1 Place the two ends parallel, but pointing in opposite directions, and half-knot them.

2 Bring each end in turn back to tuck down through the central compartment of the developing knot.

3 Finally, tuck each working end up through the bight that already encloses its own standing part.

4 Tighten the knot.

Figure-eight bend (reinforced)

This is an established alternative to the reever bend, shown opposite. Sailors once knew this knot as the Flemish bend and do not seem to have liked it much, perhaps deeming it too bulky to tie for seagoing usage.

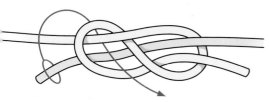

1 Bring the two ends together, parallel and facing in opposite directions, and tie a figure-eight knot in one so that it encloses the other.

2 With the other end, follow around and duplicate the knot already tied.

3 Dress and tighten the resulting knot.

Bowline (pronounced "boh-linn")

This is the fixed loop of first choice afloat for attaching a line to a ring or eye. It is also recommended for dropping over a mooring post or bollard, when it serves as a hitch ... a hitch, moreover, that can be used, removed, and reused without the need to untie and retie it.

1 Make an overhand loop and grip it firmly in the right hand (thumb underneath, fingers on top).

2 Rotate hand and forearm clockwise, in a trip-and-throw movement, to create a smaller secondary loop through which the working end projects.

3 Then take the working end around behind the standing part of the line and tuck it down through the small loop.

4 Adjust the main loop to the required size and ensure that the end is almost as long as the adjacent loop leg.

5 Tighten the knot.

EXPERT TIP
Despite this knot's sobriquet "King of Knots," there are stronger and more secure fixed loops; but it is dependable enough, while the ease with which it can be tied, untied, and cast off in crucial seconds have kept it in the repertoire of boating knots for several centuries.

Carrick bend

This bend joins large and less flexible ropes and cables. Aboard square-rigged sailing ships this bend was used to join cables that had to go around the barrel or body of a capstan.

1 Form an overhand loop in the end of one rope and lay the working end of the other rope on top of it.

2 Interweave this second working end in a locking tuck that goes under-over-under-over-under.

3 Pull on the standing parts of both ropes to capsize the flat layout into a distinctly different, but more stable and secure, configuration.

Figure-eight becket hitch

To attach a line to an eye, or the permanent seized loops known as "beckets," use this simplest of hitches.

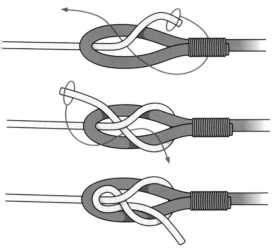

1 Pass the working end up through the loop or eye. Take it around behind the loop or eye and back to the front once more.

2 Then tuck the end beneath the initial pass.

3 Lastly, tuck the end back through itself, completing a figure-eight layout. Tighten the knot.

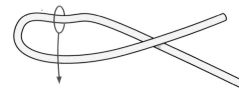

Figure-eight stopper knot

Any ropes rove through fairleads or blocks—such as jib leads and mainsheets, and perhaps halyards too—should have stopper knots tied in their ends to prevent them from pulling free. This knot is usually best for that kind of job.

1 Make a bight in the end of the line and impart half-a-twist to it.

2 Add a second half-twist in the same direction.

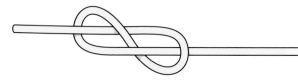

3 Tuck the working end through to complete the knot.

4 Tighten the knot by holding it and pulling on the standing part so as to wrap and trap the short end more or less at a right-angle to the rest of the rope.

5 This knot can usually be untied easily enough, but for a trivial job lasting only minutes leave a draw loop.

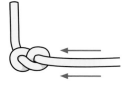

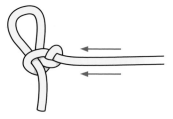

KNOT LORE
This knot is occasionally still referred to by its much older name—"Flemish knot."

Round turn and two half hitches

This go-anywhere, do-anything, knot will attach most kinds of cordage to a rail, ring, spar, post, or another rope, and withstand a pull that is steady or intermittent and from various directions. Use it when anchoring, mooring, or berthing; to secure a safety harness or other tether to a fixed point; to suspend fenders outboard; and to tow a dinghy astern.

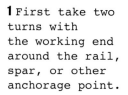

1 First take two turns with the working end around the rail, spar, or other anchorage point.

2 Next add a half hitch to the standing part of the line.

3 Then add a second identical half hitch.

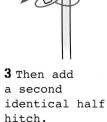

4 And finally tighten the knot.

Fisherman's bend

When the preceding round turn and two half hitches is likely to become wet and slippery, or for any other reason less reliable, resort to this more secure variant of that knot.

1 Take a turn with the working end around the ring and then insert a half hitch through that turn before tying it around the standing part of the line.

2 Add a second identical half hitch and tighten the knot.

KNOT LORE
The fisherman's bend is traditionally recommended for attaching rope warps to the rings of small anchors. It is, of course, really a hitch, and its appellation "bend" results from the fact that, in an earlier epoch, sailors spoke of "bending" a rope to a ring.

Glossary of terms

Abseil (climbing) Controlled descent of a rope.

Anchorage (climbing) Fixed and immovable point to which to belay.

Belay (climbing verb) To secure a person or object with rope.

Bend A knot that binds (or bends) two separate ropes' ends together so that they may be untied again.

Bight Any slack section of a rope or cord, especially when it forms a U-shaped tongue or open loop.

Binding A knot tied in both ends of the same short length of stuff so as to seize anything held by it.

Cable Any large rope.

Cord Cordage of less than $^1/_3$ in (10 mm) diameter, smaller than a rope.

Cordage Term for all kinds of rope, cord, and twine.

Dress To manipulate a knot into its final form before tightening it.

Fiber The smallest component in the construction of cordage made from naturally occurring materials of animal or vegetable origin.

Hitch The term for any knot that attaches a rope or cord to a fixed ring (or eye), rail, post, spar, or to another rope (or loop).

Karabiner A snap-link of aluminium or steel, with a lockable gate.

Knot The term for any cordage entanglement—accidental or deliberate—that is not a bend or hitch.

Line Any rope with a specific use (for example, guy rope, towline, laundry line).

Loop A bight with a crossing point.

Rappel *See* abseil.

Rope Cordage over $^1/_3$ in (10 mm) in diameter.

Soft-laid The flexible quality of a rope that has been manufactured with less than average tension.

Standing end The inert end of a rope or cord.

Standing part The section of any rope or cord located between the working end and the standing end.

Strand The largest element of a rope, made from contra-twisted yarns.

Stuff A common term for any kind of cordage.

Whipping A twine or thread binding to keep a cut rope's end from unravelling.

Working end The end of a rope or cord that is employed in tying knots.

Index

abseil 16, 32
Alpine butterfly loop 6, 18

bends 6, 16, 19, 22, 23, 26, 31, 32
bights 6, 7, 10, 16, 18, 20, 22, 28, 32
boating knots 24–31
bowline 8, 24

Carrick bend 6, 26
climbing knots 18, 20
constrictor knot 10
cordage 7, 8, 12, 19, 30, 32

dressing 7, 23, 32

Fields Medal 4
figure-eight becket hitch 27

figure-eight bend 23
figure-eight loop 6, 20
figure-eight stopper knot 6, 28
fisherman's bend 6, 31
Flemish bend 23
Flemish knot 29

guide knot 21

hitches 6, 24, 27, 30, 32
hoisting hitch 6, 12
Hopkins, Richard 4

Jones, Vaughan 4

karabiner 18
knot names 6-7
knot theory 4

life-support knots 18–23
loops 6, 7, 8, 10, 15, 18, 20, 24, 26, 27, 28, 32

Multipurpose knots 8–17

nooses 6, 15

overhand bend 19

rappel 16, 32
reef knot 16, 17
reever bend 22, 23
rigging 26
ring bend 19
rope 4, 6, 7, 8, 10, 12, 17,18, 20, 22, 26, 28, 30, 31, 32
round turn and two half hitches 6, 30

sheepshank 8
squeeze knot 14
standing end 7, 10, 32
standing part 7, 8, 12, 15, 16, 20, 22, 24, 26, 28, 30, 31, 32
stopper knots 6, 28

tape knot 19
Tarbuck, Ken 14
Tarbuck knot 6, 14
tying terms 6-7

webbing 19
working end 7, 10, 12, 15, 20, 22, 24, 26, 27, 28, 30, 31